CIVIL WAR
HIGHLIGHTS

THE TURNING POINT

1863

TIM COOKE

A⁺

Smart Apple Media

This edition published in 2013 by

Smart Apple Media, an imprint of Black Rabbit Books

PO Box 3263, Mankato, MN 56003

www.blackrabbitbooks.com

© 2012 Brown Bear Books Limited

Brown Bear Books Ltd.

Editorial Director: Lindsey Lowe
Managing Editor: Tim Cooke
Children's Publisher: Anne O'Daly
Picture Manager: Sophie Mortimer
Creative Director: Jeni Child

Library of Congress Cataloging-in-Publication Data
Cooke, Tim, 1961-
 The turning point, 1863 / edited by Tim Cooke.
    p. cm. -- (Civil War highlights)
 Includes bibliographical references and index.
 Summary: "Contains chronological articles describing the US Civil
War battles fought in 1863 that led to the Union victory at Gettysburg.
Includes a timeline and biographies of the War's key figures in 1863
including Abraham Lincoln, Robert E Lee, Stonewall Jackson, and Ulysses
S. Grant. Includes a quiz and other study features to help students learn
important information"--Provided by publisher.
 ISBN 978-1-59920-815-2 (library bound)
 1. United States--History--Civil War, 1861-1865--Campaigns--Juvenile
literature. I. Title.
 E470.C85 2013
 973.7'3--dc23
                        2012001168

Printed in the United States of America at Corporate Graphics,
North Mankato, Minnesota

PO1437
2-2012

9 8 7 6 5 4 3 2 1

Contents

Introduction

On January 1, 1863, President Abraham Lincoln's Emancipation Proclamation came into effect. It changed the nature of the war: It was now a struggle against slavery.

The Proclamation declared that all slaves in Confederate territory were now free. Although slavery had been one of the major causes of the war, this was the first time freeing the slaves had become a formal war aim of the Union. It was now highly unlikely that the Confederacy would be recognized by any European powers. No major country would support an open struggle to preserve slavery.

On the battlefield, Confederate commander Robert E. Lee and his senior general, Thomas "Stonewall" Jackson, proved a match for the Union Army of the Potomac in the early part of the year. Jackson's death at the Battle of Chancellorsville was a blow to Confederate morale and its battlefield effectiveness.

Abraham Lincoln (*left*) reads a draft of his Emancipation Proclamation to his cabinet.

General Ulysses S. Grant uses a telescope to survey the action during the Union siege of Vicksburg.

The Union renewed its attempts to capture the Mississippi River by besieging Port Hudson and the key city of Vicksburg. Lee decided to invade the North again. At the start of July 1863 he met the Union Army of the Potomac at Gettysburg, Pennsylvania. In the war's biggest battle, the Union forces halted Lee's advance, and ended the Confederacy's ability to mount strategic offensives. From now on, Lee would be on the defensive.

In this book

The Turning Point describes the major engagements that led to Gettysburg and the actions that followed. It also examines some of the most influential individuals of this crucial year. A timeline that runs across the bottom of the pages throughout the book traces the course of the war on the battlefield and other developments in North America and the rest of the world. At the back of the book is a Need to Know feature, which will help you relate subjects to your studies at school.

Setting Free the Slaves

President Abraham Lincoln's Emancipation Proclamation came into effect on January 1, 1863. It set free America's slaves—and changed the whole nature of the Civil War.

A slave's life (left) is contrasted with scenes of freedmen (right) after the war by Thomas Nast.

Lincoln had issued a preliminary version of the Proclamation in September 1862. It said that from January 1, 1863, all people held as slaves in the rebel states were free and could not be enslaved again. The proclamation had no practical effect for

1861 January–March

CIVIL WAR

JANUARY 2, SOUTH CAROLINA Fort Johnson in Charleston Harbor is occupied by Confederate troops.

JANUARY 5, ALABAMA Alabama troops seize forts Morgan and Gaines, giving Confederate forces control of Mobile Bay.

JANUARY 9, MISSISSIPPI Leaders vote to leave the Union. Mississippi is the second state to join the Confederacy.

JANUARY 10, FLORIDA Florida leaves the Union.

JANUARY 11, ALABAMA Alabama leaves the Union.

OTHER EVENTS

JANUARY 15, UNITED STATES Engineer Elisha Otis invents the safety elevator.

JANUARY 29, UNITED STATES Kansas joins the Union as the 34th state.

January

slaves in the Confederacy, of course. Its importance was more symbolic. It changed the Civil War from a struggle to save the Union; now it was also a war to free the slaves. Lincoln's Secretary of the Navy, Gideon Welles, called it "a landmark in history."

The Union began to recruit black troops at the end of 1862; numbers grew quickly after January 1, 1863.

Lincoln himself had always said that his main duty as president was to hold together the Union by stopping the rebellion in the South, not to free the slaves. But Lincoln and other politicians knew that the issue of slavery would eventually have to be addressed. It lay at the heart of the war.

Lincoln's announcement

By the middle of 1862, the Union faced a difficult situation. There had been no quick victory in the war. Instead, the armies of North and South had fought themselves to a standstill. But Lincoln needed to act. The Union's armies desperately needed recruits to replace the men they had lost. Meanwhile, the South's armies were supported by slavery. Slaves provided the labor that allowed white Southerners to go to fight. Lincoln also feared that Britain might recognize the Confederate government.

On September 17, 1862, the Union won a strategic victory at the Battle of Antietam (Sharpsburg) when it halted the Confederate invasion of the North. Lincoln judged that there

JANUARY 19, GEORGIA
Georgia votes to leave the Union.

JANUARY 26, LOUISIANA
Louisiana becomes the sixth state to leave the Union.

FEBRUARY 4, ALABAMA
Leaders from the South meet in the state capital, Montgomery. They choose Jefferson Davis of Mississippi as their president and write a constitution for the Confederate States of America.

FEBRUARY 7, ALABAMA/MISSISSIPPI
The Choctaw Indian Nation forms an alliance with the South. Other Indian tribes follow later.

FEBRUARY, UNITED STATES
The first moving picture system is patented.

MARCH, RUSSIA
Czar Alexander II abolishes serfdom (a form of slavery).

February   March

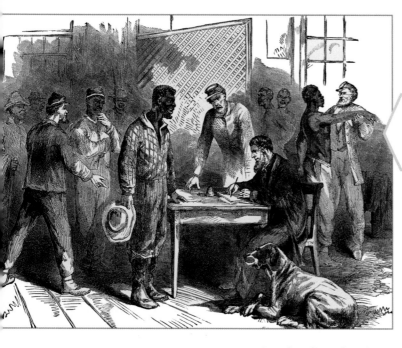

African Americans wait at a recruitment center to volunteer for the Union army.

was now enough public support for freeing the slaves to make emancipation a national policy. On September 22, he issued his preliminary proclamation.

Lincoln gave the Southern states an ultimatum. If they did not rejoin the Union by the end of the year, their slaves would be declared free. Not a single Confederate state complied. Freeing the South's slaves therefore became a major Union war aim.

WAITING FOR THE RIGHT MOMENT

Lincoln did not want to make the proclamation while the North was weak. The Union's tactical victory on September 17, 1862, at the Battle of Antietam (Sharpsburg) was the breakthrough he needed. He issued the proclamation five days later.

Contrasting reactions

In the South, the proclamation caused outrage. President Jefferson Davis accused Lincoln of trying to start a slave revolt in the Confederacy. If the slaves began an insurrection, he warned, they would face "extermination." Davis also tried to discourage the Union from recruiting black soldiers. He said that "all negro slaves captured in arms" and their white officers would be tried under Confederate laws.

In the North, meanwhile, the proclamation was widely welcomed. Abolitionists, African Americans, and others were quick to congratulate Lincoln. The former slave Frederick Douglass, who was a leading abolitionist, wrote: "We are all liberated ... by the Emancipation Proclamation.... The white man is liberated, the black man is liberated, the brave men now fighting ... against rebels and traitors are now liberated."

1861
April–June

CIVIL WAR

APRIL 12, SOUTH CAROLINA Confederates fire on Fort Sumter in Charleston Harbor in the first shots of the Civil War.

APRIL 15, THE NORTH President Lincoln calls for 75,000 recruits across the North to fight the South.

APRIL 19, WASHINGTON, D.C. President Lincoln declares a naval blockade of Southern states.

APRIL 19, BALTIMORE Mayor George Brown bans Union troops from the city after they are attacked by an angry pro-Confederate mob.

OTHER EVENTS

APRIL, EGYPT A search party sets out from Cairo to find the explorers John Speke and James Grant, who have gone missing while looking for the source of the Nile River.

April

Other abolitionists were not as pleased, however. They were disappointed that the proclamation only freed slaves in areas under Confederate control. It said nothing about the slave states that had stayed in the Union, or about Southern territory in Union hands. In practice, however, slaves were freed in territories that fell to the Union and in other regions.

Some people were also disappointed that Lincoln had not made a fuller commitment to racial equality. The proclamation was not based on principles but on the military needs of the Union. The final proclamation of January 1, 1863, decreed that freed slaves could now join the Union army to fight against the South and slavery.

Beginning of a process

The Emancipation Proclamation began the process of freeing the slaves. It gave the Union cause in the war a moral force. It made more troops available. It also ensured that no European country would intervene in the war. They did not want to oppose a crusade against slavery.

The end of slavery only came with the Thirteenth Amendment to the Constitution in December 1865. However, African Americans still had many battles to fight before they would become truly free.

An elderly man reads a newspaper headline about the Proclamation.

AFRICAN AMERICAN SOLDIERS

The Union only started actively recruiting African Americans in spring 1863. The final Emancipation Proclamation of January 1 had decreed that freed slaves "will be received into the armed service of the United States to garrison forts, positions, stations...." This signaled a major change in policy, because since 1861 the Union army had been turning away free black volunteers. From spring 1863, free blacks and former slaves rushed to join the Union army. They were determined to help bury slavery, to defeat the Confederates, and to earn full citizenship. By 1865 the Union army had enlisted 180,000 black soldiers.

APRIL 23, VIRGINIA Major General Robert E. Lee becomes commander of land and naval forces in Virginia.

APRIL 27, WASHINGTON, D.C. Abraham Lincoln suspends "habeus corpus," a law that protects individuals from being arrested.

MAY 9, GREAT BRITAIN Britain announces it will remain neutral in the Civil War.

MAY 20, NORTH CAROLINA North Carolina is the last state to leave the Union.

JUNE 20, VIRGINIA West Virginia is unhappy at Virginia's decision to leave the Union. It breaks from the Confederacy and is admitted into the Union.

APRIL, AUSTRALIA Robert Burke and William Wills, who led the first expedition across Australia, narrowly miss a rendezvous with their colleagues; Burke and Wills will die in the Outback.

JUNE, WASHINGTON, D.C. "Aeronaut" Thaddeus Lowe demonstrates his hot-air balloon for President Abraham Lincoln.

May   June

Guerrilla War

A number of armed bands took fighting into their own hands in the South. These guerrillas attacked Union settlements or army positions, often with the backing of the government.

This illustration shows a small party of Mosby's Rangers in the Shenandoah Valley.

These guerrillas were known as partisans. They were led by men such as William C. Quantrill and William "Bloody Bill" Anderson. They had a reputation for viciousness that made them highly feared in the states near the border.

1861
July–September

CIVIL WAR

JULY 2, WISCONSIN Union forces push back Confederates near Hainesville in the Battle of Hoke's Run.

JULY 6, CUBA The Confederate raiding ship CSS *Sumter* captures seven vessels in Cuban waters.

JULY 21, VIRGINIA The first major battle of the war is fought at Manassas/First Bull Run. Confederates led by Pierre G.T. Beauregard defeat General Irvin McDowell's larger Union army.

OTHER EVENTS

JULY, UNITED STATES The Pony Express arrives in San Francisco, beginning a cross-country mail service.

JULY, UNITED STATES Congress approves the printing of the first dollar bills, known as "greenbacks."

July

John S. Mosby

One of the most notorious guerrillas was John Singleton Mosby. He led a band of partisan rangers in an area of Virginia east of the Blue Ridge Mountains that became known as "Mosby's Confederacy." Mosby and his men have acquired a mythical status over the years, especially in the South.

Mosby had served in the Confederate army before resigning to form his band in northern Virginia. In April 1862 the Confederate government authorized partisan rangers to fight independently behind enemy lines.

Mosby's Rangers

Mosby's unit grew until the Confederate government finally gave it an official name: the 43rd Battalion Virginia Cavalry. Most people knew it as "Mosby's Rangers." As the leader, Mosby planned and led raids on Union outposts in northern counties near Washington, D.C. After raids, his rangers melted back into the local population. From 1863 to 1865 Mosby is thought to have captured more than 1,000 Union prisoners, more than 1,000 horses, large amounts of weapons and ammunition, and hundreds of thousands of dollars in cash.

Although the "Gray Ghost," as Mosby was known, controlled "Mosby's Confederacy," his actions did not change the outcome of the war. Unwilling to surrender, he disbanded his partisan rangers on April 21, 1865, 11 days after Robert E. Lee's surrender at Appomattox.

FAMOUS RAIDS

Two of Mosby's raids serve as examples of his daring. In a raid on March 8, 1863, Mosby seized as a prisoner a Union general, Edwin Stoughton, commander of the garrison at Fairfax, Virginia. The raid cemented Mosby's fame in both the North and the South.

The 1864 "Greenback Raid" was equally bold. At dawn on October 14 Mosby's men stopped a Union passenger train on the Baltimore and Ohio Railroad just west of Harpers Ferry, Virginia. The rangers stole $173,000 in U.S. currency from the guard before setting the train on fire.

Partisan leader John S. Mosby was 27 at the outbreak of the Civil War.

AUGUST 10, MISSOURI
The Battle of Wilson's Creek is the first major battle on the Mississippi River; it sees the first death of a Union general, Nathaniel Lyon.

SEPTEMBER 3, KENTUCKY
Confederate forces invade Kentucky, ending its neutrality.

SEPTEMBER 12–15, WEST VIRGINIA
General Robert E. Lee's Confederate forces are beaten at the Battle of Cheat Mountain Summit.

SEPTEMBER 19, KENTUCKY
The Battle of Barbourville sees Confederates raid an empty Union guerrilla training base.

AUGUST, UNITED STATES
The U.S. Government introduces the first income tax to raise funds for the war.

August   September

Battle of Chancellorsville

Confederate commander Robert E. Lee has a reputation as one of the outstanding generals of the Civil War. At Chancellorsville, his tactics allowed him to defeat a Union army of twice the size.

"Three Heroes" shows (from left to right) Stonewall Jackson, Robert E. Lee, and J.E.B. Stuart.

At the start of 1863, President Abraham Lincoln had appointed yet another new commander to the Army of the Potomac to replace General Ambrose Burnside. Lincoln wanted the Union to go on the offensive again. The man he appointed—

1861
October–December

CIVIL WAR

OCTOBER 21, KENTUCKY 7,000 Union troops defeat Confederates at the Battle of Camp Wildcat on Wildcat Mountain.

OCTOBER 21, MISSOURI Union attempts to cross the Potomac River at Harrison's Island fail in the Battle of Ball's Bluff.

OCTOBER 21, MISSOURI The Union controls southeastern Missouri after the Battle of Fredericktown.

NOVEMBER 7, MISSOURI Ulysses S. Grant's Union forces defeat Confederates at the Battle of Belmont.

OTHER EVENTS

OCTOBER 22, UNITED STATES The first telegraph line is completed linking the east and west coasts.

NOVEMBER 1, UNITED STATES Jefferson Davis is elected as president of the Confederacy.

October   November

General Joseph Hooker—promised to do just that, as suggested by his popular nickname, "Fighting Joe."

In December 1862 the Union had tried to capture the city of Fredericksburg, Virginia, on the Rappahannock River. The battle had been a costly failure. Since then, the Union Army of the Potomac and the Confederate Army of Northern Virginia had faced one another across the Rappahannock.

A new plan

By the spring of 1863, Hooker had come up with a new plan. He did not want to repeat the disastrous frontal attacks on the Confederate position on the high ground above Frdericksburg. Instead, he went against military theory and divided his army. He left John Sedgwick at Fredericksburg with 40,000 men to hold the Confederates in their positions. Hooker himself led 75,000 men upstream. He planned to cross the river and make a wide sweep to attack Lee from behind.

Robert E. Lee leads his troops at the Battle of Chancellorsville, Virginia, in May 1863.

By April 30 Hooker's troops had forded the river. They were in an area of tangled woodland known as the Wilderness. The center of their position lay on a crossroads at Chancellorsville, Virginia. But now Hooker's plan began to go wrong.

NOVEMBER 8, CUBA
British steamer *Trent* is stopped by Union warship *San Jacinto* in an action that breaks international law, as Britain is not a combatant in the Civil War.

NOVEMBER 8, KENTUCKY
The Battle of Ivy Mountain, also known as Ivy Creek, sees Union soldiers push Confederates back into Virginia.

DECEMBER 20, VIRGINIA Union troops defeat Confederate cavalry under J.E.B. "Jeb" Stuart in the Battle of Dranesville.

NOVEMBER 19, UNITED STATES
Julia Howe writes the first verses of "The Battle Hymn of the Republic."

DECEMBER 14, GREAT BRITAIN Prince Albert, the husband of Queen Victoria, dies, plunging his wife into a long period of mourning.

General Joseph Hooker failed to live up to his promise that he would "whip Bobby Lee."

Realizing that Hooker was trying a flanking march, Lee had begun to prepare his defenses. On April 29 he sent two brigades to make a reconnaissance of the enemy threat. Once they had confirmed Hooker's presence at Chancellorsville, Lee went on the attack. Like Hooker, Lee divided his forces. He marched 50,000 men to meet Hooker. Meanwhile, Jubal A. Early and 10,000 men stayed on the heights to protect Fredericksburg.

At noon on May 1, Confederates began to attack the lead Union divisions. The attack took Hooker completely by surprise. Despite his reputation, the Union commander lost his nerve. Halting his advance, he ordered his forces to take up defensive positions back at Chancellorsville.

A bold maneuver

Surprise had given Lee the initiative, and he set out to take advantage of it. Early on May 2, he sent Thomas J. "Stonewall" Jackson and 28,000 men on a 12-mile (19-km) march to strike Hooker's right flank. Lee and his remaining troops faced three Union corps. Lee had now divided his army not once but twice. It was one of the boldest moves of the whole war.

Jackson's march took all day, but at 6:00 P.M. he attacked the Union XI Corps, which broke and ran. Only nightfall saved

TACTICAL GENIUS

Robert E. Lee is widely seen as the greatest commander of the war. His actions at Chancellorsville, when he divided his forces and maneuvered them to fight on two fronts, helped earn his reputation. The Union commander Winfield Scott called him "the greatest military genius in America."

1862
January–March

CIVIL WAR

JANUARY 18, ARIZONA
The Confederate Territory of Arizona is formed from part of what was the old Territory of New Mexico.

FEBRUARY 6, TENNESSEE
Union General Ulysses S. Grant takes the Confederate Fort Henry. The Tennessee River is now under Union control as far as Alabama.

FEBRUARY 16, TENNESSEE
Grant's troops take Fort Donelson; 15,000 Southerners surrender.

OTHER EVENTS

FEBRUARY, UNITED STATES "The Battle Hymn of the Republic" is published and quickly becomes a popular marching song in the Union.

January   February

Hooker's army. That evening, however, Lee also suffered a huge blow. Returning from a patrol, Jackson was accidentally shot and fatally wounded by his own men.

J.E.B. Stuart took over for Jackson and reopened the attack the next day, while Lee struck from the south. The Confederates pushed the Union line back toward the river. Hooker faced total defeat.

Help was on its way, however. Early's defenders at Fredericksburg had been unable to hold Sedgwick's Union troops, who were now advancing to Hooker's aid. On May 4, Lee turned to face Sedgwick. He halted him at Salem Church.

Hooker withdrew across the river on the night of May 5. Defeat had cost more than 17,000 men. Lee's 12,800 casualties included Stonewall Jackson, who died a few days later.

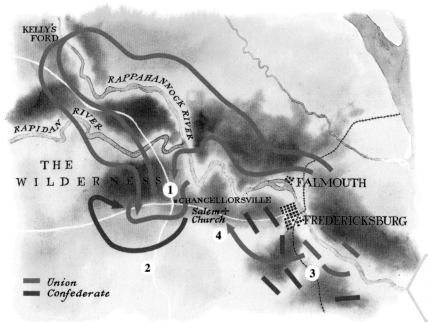

This map shows the main positions in the battle.

BATTLE DETAILS

1. The Union army marched north, crossed the river, and took up positions around the Chancellorsville crossroads.

2. On May 2 Lee divided his forces for a second time. He sent Jackson on a flanking march to attack the Union right, which fled.

3. On May 3, as fighting went on at Chancellorsville, Union forces drove the Confederates away from Fredericksburg and advanced to Salem Church.

4. Lee turned his army around to stop this advance and defeated the Union troops. On May 5 and 6 Hooker's Union forces retreated across the river.

FEBRUARY 25, TENNESSEE With the loss of forts Henry and Donelson, Nashville is the first Confederate state capital to fall to Union forces.

MARCH 6–8, ARKANSAS The Confederates are defeated at the Battle of Pea Ridge, the largest battle on Arkansas soil.

MARCH 8–9, VIRGINIA The Battle of Hampton Roads sees Confederate and Union ironclads fight to a standstill.

MARCH 17, VIRGINIA The Union Army of the Potomac sails to Fort Monroe to begin the Peninsular Campaign.

MARCH, EAST AFRICA Zanzibar becomes an independent nation.

MARCH 10, UNITED STATES The first U.S. paper money goes into circulation.

March

Thomas J. Jackson

The death of "Stonewall" Jackson at Chancellorsville was a devastating loss for the South. Robert E. Lee had lost one of his boldest and most able commanders.

Jackson (at right, on horse) falls in his saddle after being shot by his own men at Chancellorsville.

Thomas J. Jackson had earned his famous nickname, "Stonewall," at the First Battle of Bull Run (Manassas) in July 1861. In the afternoon's fighting, the Confederate line had been in danger of collapsing in the face of a ferocious Union

1862
April–June

CIVIL WAR

APRIL 6–7, TENNESSEE In the Battle of Shiloh Ulysses S. Grant narrowly defeats Confederate forces, with heavy losses on both sides.

APRIL 12, GEORGIA Union agent James Ambrose steals a Confederate train on the Western & Atlantic Railroad. He is captured and hanged.

APRIL 29, THE SOUTH The Confederacy passes a conscription act forcing men aged 18 to 50 to enlist in the army; many farms go into decline as farmers join up.

APRIL 29, LOUISIANA The Union occupation of New Orleans opens access to the rest of Louisiana and the Mississippi Valley.

OTHER EVENTS

APRIL 8, UNITED STATES Inventor John D. Lynde patents the first aerosol spray.

April

assault. In the center of the action, Jackson's brigade of Virginians stood firm. General Barnard Bee rallied his own troops by pointing out Jackson's example: "There is Jackson, standing like a stone wall!"

A bold commander

Jackson graduated from the U.S. Military Academy at West Point, fought in the Mexican War (1846–1848), and taught at the Virginia Military Institute. When the Civil War began, he joined the Confederate army out of loyalty to his home state, Virginia.

After Bull Run Jackson was promoted to major general. He campaigned in the Shenandoah Valley in spring 1862, defeating Union generals with larger forces. Jackson then joined Robert E. Lee in the Army of Northern Virginia. He was vital to Lee's tactics at Second Bull Run (Manassas) on August 27, at Antietam (Sharpsburg) on September 17, and at Fredericksburg on December 13. In October 1862 Jackson was promoted to lieutenant general. Lee gave him comand of II Corps of the Army of Northern Virginia.

"Stonewall" Jackson became a hero because of his aggressive tactics and speed against the enemy.

Friendly fire

The Battle of Chancellorsville in May 1863 was Jackson's greatest victory. After a bold maneuver, he attacked and routed a Union corps. But the day ended in tragedy: Jackson was accidentally shot when his own men mistook his party for Union cavalry. Jackson's arm was amputated but he caught pneumonia and died eight days later, on May 10, 1863. His death caused widespread mourning throughout the South.

MAY 31, VIRGINIA
The Battle of Fair Oaks (Seven Pines) is drawn. Union losses are 5,050 and Confederate losses are 6,150.

JUNE 1, VIRGINIA
General Robert E. Lee takes command of the Army of Northern Virgina after General Joseph Johnston is wounded.

JUNE 12, VIRGINIA
J.E.B. Stuart and 1,200 cavalry raid the Union camp outside Richmond, taking 165 prisoners.

JUNE 25, VIRGINIA
The first battle of the Seven Days' Campaign—the Battle of Oak Grove—sees McClellan's Union forces halted near Richmond.

MAY 5, MEXICO
A Mexican army defeats an invading French force in the Battle of Puebla.

MAY 20, UNITED STATES
The Homestead Act makes millions of acres of Western land available to settlers.

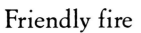

May   June

Fall of Port Hudson

The Union plan to win control of the Mississippi had begun with the capture of New Orleans in April 1862. The next logical target was the heavily fortified Confederate position at Port Hudson.

This contemporary painting shows Union gunboats bombing Port Hudson in May 1863.

The war in the West was focused on the Mississippi River. In early 1863 Union General Ulysses S. Grant was still attempting to capture the vital city of Vicksburg on the river, which linked the eastern and western parts of the Confederacy.

1862
July–September

CIVIL WAR

JULY 1, WASHINGTON, D.C. The Union introduces an Internal Revenue Act, imposing a tax on income to raise money to pay for the war.

JULY 13, WASHINGTON, D.C. President Lincoln reads a draft of the Emancipation Proclamation to his cabinet.

JULY 17, THE NORTH The Confiscation Act and Militia Act come into force, opening the way for the creation of black regiments of freed slaves.

AUGUST 29, VIRGINIA The Second Battle of Bull Run (Manassas) begins.

OTHER EVENTS

JULY 4, GREAT BRITAIN Lewis Carroll makes up the story that will become *Alice in Wonderland* to amuse a young friend.

JULY 14, UNITED STATES Congress introduces the Medal of Honor for valor in the military services.

July   August

In order to move upriver toward Vicksburg, Union General Nathaniel P. Banks planned to capture Port Hudson. The city was heavily reinforced. Its commander, General Franklin Gardner, had constructed fortified positions facing both the river and the land.

A naval attack

Banks's first purely naval attempt to capture Port Hudson failed. So, on May 11, 1863, Banks began a stronger attack. He led 30,000 Union land and naval troops out of Baton Rouge. Gardner had only 3,500 defenders, but he used them so well that he was able to hold off Union assaults for two weeks.

Confederate guns fire on Union warships. Port Hudson fell on July 8, 1863, after a 47-day siege.

After suffering high casualties, Banks halted the attacks in late May. Instead, he decided to lay siege to Port Hudson by starving it into submission. Gardner now had no hope of victory: no other Confederate forces were in a position to come to his aid. Gradually the food, medicine, and ammunition inside the town ran out. Nevertheless, Gardner refused to surrender until July 4, when news came that Vicksburg had itself given up and surrendered.

Although he had ultimately been defeated, Gardner had tied up more than 30,000 Union troops who could have been used at the Siege of Vicksburg. The two victories secured Union control of the Mississippi River for the remainder of the war.

AUGUST 30, VIRGINIA
Confederate Robert E. Lee defeats the Union army at Bull Run. His casualties stand at 9,500, while Union losses are 14,500.

SEPTEMBER 17, MARYLAND
The Battle of Antietam ends in a draw after heavy losses on both sides: Lee's Army of Northern Virginia suffers 10,000 casualties; the Union Army of the Potomac loses 12,400 dead, wounded, or missing.

SEPTEMBER 22, WASHINGTON, D.C.
Lincoln issues a preliminary Emancipation Proclamation.

SEPTEMBER 24, TENNESSEE
Union General William Sherman orders the destruction of every house in Randolph in revenge for Confederate shelling of his steamboats.

AUGUST 18, UNITED STATES An uprising by young Sioux Indians in Minnesota leaves more than 800 white settlers dead.

September

Battle of Brandy Station

For the first years of the Civil War, the South's cavalry forces were superior to those of the North. At Brandy Station, however, Union horsemen proved more than a match for their opponents.

A Union cavalry officer at winter quarters near Brandy Station, 1863–1864.

The clash at Brandy Station, Virginia, on June 9, 1863, was the largest cavalry battle ever fought in North America. It reflected how cavalry and cavalry tactics had changed since the start of the war, particularly in the North. But the battle had no

1862
October–December

CIVIL WAR

OCTOBER 3, MISSISSIPPI
A Union army defeats the Confederates in the Battle of Corinth.

OCTOBER 11, VIRGINIA
The Confederate Congress passes an unpopular draft law that exempts anyone owning more than 20 slaves—the wealthiest part of society—from military service.

NOVEMBER 7, WASHINGTON, D.C.
Lincoln fires George B. McClellan as commander of the Army of the Potomac and appoints Ambrose E. Burnside in his place.

OTHER EVENTS

OCTOBER 8, PRUSSIA Otto von Bismarck becomes minister-president of Prussia; he uses his position to mastermind the unification of Germany.

NOVEMBER 4, UNITED STATES
Richard Gatling patents the machine gun that is named for him: the Gatling gun.

October   November

Union wagons near Brandy Station. Each army was followed by hundreds of wagons carrying essential supplies.

particular strategic influence on the course of the war. For the Confederate commander Robert E. Lee, in fact, it was a distraction. It interrupted his plans to invade the North for a second time in less than a year.

The fighting begins

The battle began on the morning of June 9. Two divisions of General Alfred Pleasanton's Union Cavalry Corps crossed the Rappahannock River. Commanded by John Buford and David M. Gregg, respectively, the Union divisions intended to meet up near Brandy Station and attack Confederates known to be in the area.

Buford's division surprised William Jones' Confederate cavalry in their camps near the river and attacked. Jones and his men hurriedly set up a defensive position, which they held until reinforcements arrived. In the intense fighting, cavalrymen on both sides dismounted and fought as infantry from the shelter of stone walls.

DECEMBER 7, TENNESSEE
Confederates defeat Union troops at the Battle of Hartsville, opening up parts of western Tennessee and Kentucky.

DECEMBER 13–14, VIRGINIA
Burnside is beaten back in the Battle of Fredericksburg, with the loss of 6,500 Union troops.

DECEMBER 31, TENNESSEE
Union troops triumph in the Battle of Murfreesboro, taking Kentucky and increasing their hold on Tennessee.

DECEMBER 30, UNITED STATES
Lincoln reads his Emancipation Proclamation to his cabinet for comments.

DECEMBER 31, UNITED STATES
Lincoln signs an act admitting West Virginia to the Union.

This contemporary drawing shows the 1st Maine Cavalry fighting in June 1863.

J.E.B. "JEB" STUART

As well as being an inspirational commander, J.E.B. Stuart was a good horseman known for his skill at reconnaissance and his use of cavalry to attack Union troops. Brandy Station marked a low point in his brilliant career.

Gregg's 5,000 men had meanwhile crossed the river several miles to the south and split into two groups. They advanced toward Fleetwood Hill, the headquarters of the Confederate cavalry commander J.E.B. "Jeb" Stuart. Jones's Confederates also fell back to Fleetwood Hill, pursued by Buford.

As the cavalry became concentrated on Fleetwood Hill, a remarkable battle began. Thousands of horsemen made a series of mass charges and countercharges, but neither side gained the upper hand. As the afternoon went on, casualties mounted. Finally the Union forces began to withdraw. First, a series of Confederate counterattacks pushed the northernmost units back across the Rappahannock. They were followed by the Union forces closer to Fleetwood Hill.

Incomplete victory

By most criteria, Jeb Stuart had won a clear victory. His cavalry were left in possession of the battlefield. They had held their positions and caused almost twice as many enemy casualties (866) as they suffered themselves (485). But that was not the whole story. Stuart had been completely taken by surprise by the bold Union attack. And even though they may have lost the battle, Pleasanton's Union cavalrymen had fought well. There had clearly been a significant improvement

1863 January–March

CIVIL WAR

JANUARY 1, WASHINGTON, D.C.
The Emancipation Proclamation comes into effect, ruling that slaves in the South are free. The Civil War is now a war for the abolition of slavery, as well as a struggle to preserve the Union.

JANUARY 20–22, VIRGINIA
The Union Army of the Potomac tries to cross the Rappahannock River but turns back as rain turns the ground to mud.

OTHER EVENTS

JANUARY 1, UNITED STATES
The Homestead Act comes into law, encouraging western migration by granting land to farmers.

JANUARY 10, GREAT BRITAIN
The world's first underground railroad line opens in London.

FEBRUARY 3, UNITED STATES
Newspaper editor Samuel Clemens first uses the pen name by which he will become famous: Mark Twain.

January   February

in the skill of the Union cavalry. Stuart's reputation had taken a blow, meanwhile. Some historians believe that he tried to redeem himself by taking risks during the later Gettysburg campaign—risks that helped bring a Confederate defeat.

Union cavalry

For the North, the Battle of Brandy Station was reassuring evidence of the improvement in their cavalry. Earlier in the war, Union cavalry units had suffered from poor leadership and training. Many of the recruits were from the North's towns and cities. Some only learned to ride after they had enlisted. In contrast, cavalrymen from the more rural South were often expert horsemen. Also, many Confederate cavalrymen fought in their own local areas, which was a clear advantage in an age before many detailed maps existed.

An 1863 Union recruitment poster offers a bounty for new recruits.

Brandy Station showed that the gap between Union and Confederate cavalry units had narrowed. In fact, it was clear that the Union cavalry were better armed and supplied than their enemy, thanks to the North's ability to produce more food for horses, more equipment, and more weapons and ammunition. The fighting spirit of Union cavalrymen was never in doubt, either, and leaders such as Buford turned their units into successful combat forces. After June 1863 the cavalry played a growing role in the Union war effort.

HORSES IN THE CIVIL WAR

Brandy Station showed the importance of cavalry in the war, but horses were not only used for cavalrymen. Both sides relied on horses to pull their artillery guns and ammunition. Scouts rode horses to observe the enemy. Officers in all branches of the army rode horses. And armies relied on horses to help transport supplies. When the Union Army of the Potomac invaded Virginia in 1864, its wagon train of supplies was 5 miles (8 km) long, with 500 horses. For commanders on both sides, maintaining a supply of horses and a supply of food for them was a priority. In all, some 1.5 million horses and mules were killed during the war.

MARCH 3, WASHINGTON, D.C.
The Union introduces the National Conscription Act, obliging men to join the army or pay $300 to hire a substitute.

MARCH 3, THE SOUTH
The Confederacy introduces an unpopular Impressment Act that allows army officers to take food from farmers at set rates.

FEBRUARY 24, UNITED STATES
Arizona is organized as a territory of the United States.

MARCH 3, UNITED STATES
The territory of Idaho is created.

March

Siege of Vicksburg

The capture of Vicksburg, Mississippi, was vital if the Union was to regain control of the Mississippi River. Ulysses S. Grant's campaign to take the city lasted eight months.

During the siege, Union attackers and Confederate soldiers hurl hand grenades at each other.

Vicksburg was essential to the South. From its position on the Mississippi it dominated trade in a vast area between New Orleans and Memphis. The Union had captured both New Orleans and Memphis by the middle of 1862, however. That left

1863 April–June

CIVIL WAR

APRIL 2, VIRGINIA "Bread riots" break out in the Confederacy over the high price of food; the worst riots are in Richmond.

APRIL 17, MISSISSIPPI Union cavalry raids Mississippi, tearing up railroad lines. Soldiers ride south to the Union city of Baton Rouge, Louisiana.

MAY 2–4, VIRGINIA The Confederate Army of Northern Virginia defeats the Union Army of the Potomac at the Battle of Chancellorsville; however, Confederate commander "Stonewall" Jackson is shot by one of his own men and dies.

MAY 14, MISSISSIPPI Union troops capture Jackson, the fourth state capital to fall to Union troops.

OTHER EVENTS

MAY 22, UNITED STATES The War Department establishes the Bureau of Colored Troops.

April   May

Vicksburg as the only link between the eastern and western halves of the Confederacy. If the Union could capture Vicksburg it would not just consolidate its position in the Mississippi Valley, but it would also split the Confederacy in two. President Jefferson Davis ordered that Vicksburg must be saved at all costs.

Supplies for the Union Army of the Cumberland. It was the main force in Tennessee from 1862 to 1863.

The Union plan

Vicksburg stood on high bluffs on a loop in the Mississippi and was a formidable obstacle. Ulysses S. Grant had planned a two-part assault on the heavily fortified city from the north. In December 1862 General William T. Sherman sailed down the Mississippi. Grant himself intended to march overland to Vicksburg from Memphis. However, Grant had to abandon his advance when his main supply base was destroyed by Confederate raiders on December 20. Sherman went ahead with an attempt to capture the high bluffs north of the city. When he failed, he withdrew on December 29.

The Mississippi River lay between Grant and Vicksburg, protecting the city to the west. He therefore planned to lead his army through the swamps along the river out of sight of the city's defenses, ferry it across the Mississippi, and attack from the high ground to the east. During the winter he tried three

MAY 18, MISSISSIPPI
Union armies begin the siege of Vicksburg.

JUNE 9, VIRGINIA
The Battle of Brandy Station ends in a Confederate victory.

JUNE 14, VIRGINIA
The Battle of Winchester is another Confederate victory.

JUNE 16, VIRGINIA
Lee orders the Army of Northern Virginia across the Potomac River to invade the North for a second time.

JUNE 28, WASHINGTON, D.C.
Lincoln replaces General Joseph Hooker as commander of the Army of the Potomac with General George Meade, whom he hopes will be more aggressive.

JUNE 7, MEXICO French troops capture Mexico City; the French want to begin a colony while Americans are distracted by the war.

JUNE 20, UNITED STATES
West Virginia is admitted to the Union following a presidential proclamation.

June

The besieging Union army blow a crater in Fort Hill, part of the defenses around Vicksburg.

MISSISSIPPI RIVER

If the Union gained control of the Mississippi River, the Confederacy would be cut in half and would struggle to survive. The Confederacy needed to defend the vital transportation route and rich agricultural lands of the lower Mississippi Valley. They fortified strategic points along the river with forts and mines.

times to move his army behind Vicksburg using river transport. All three attempts failed.

Grant's new plan

By the start of the spring, Grant had accepted that he would have to change his tactics. He now sent his army some 30 miles (48 km) south from Vicksburg to cut a way through the swamps to the river. Under cover of night, Union gunboats sailed past the Confederate guns at Vicksburg to meet up with Grant's army. On April 30 the gunboats ferried the Union forces across the river. Sherman kept the Confederates busy with a diversionary attack north of the city.

Grant did not turn to Vicksburg immediately. Instead, he headed east, where he drove the Confederate army of Joseph E. Johnston back to Jackson. Grant did not want Johnston to join up with John C. Pemberton's army at Vicksburg.

Grant finally turned west. As he advanced on Vicksburg, the Confederates advanced to meet him. Grant defeated Pemberton at Champion's Hill on May 16 and again the next day at Big Black River. Pemberton retreated into Vicksburg. Grant attempted to take the city twice, but it was so well fortified that Grant realized it did not need to surrender until its supplies ran out. On 22 May Grant settled in for a siege.

1863 July–September

CIVIL WAR

JULY 1–3, PENNSYLVANNIA
The Battle of Gettysburg yields over 20,000 casualties on each side in a decisive Union victory that marks a turning point in the war.

JULY 4, MISSISSIPPI
The fall of Vicksburg to the Union splits the Confederacy in two.

JULY 13, NEW YORK
Antidraft riots erupt across the North; in the worst, in New York City, African Americans are attacked and draft offices burned.

JULY 18, SOUTH CAROLINA
The 54th Massachusetts Volunteer Infantry, a black Union unit, fails in a courageous attack on Fort Wagner.

OTHER EVENTS

JULY 1, SOUTH AMERICA
The Dutch abolish slavery in their colony in Suriname.

JULY, CAMBODIA French writers reveal for the first time the existence of the remarkable ruined city of Angkor in the Cambodian jungle.

July

Life under siege

Grant's men set about cutting off Vicksburg from the outside. They surrounded it with 15 miles (24 km) of trenches. Shells rained down on the city around the clock from the Union's 220 heavy guns. Inside Vicksburg civilians suffered as much as the soldiers. Many took refuge in caves dug out of the hillsides. Food soon began to run out, and by late June mule and rat meat was all that was left.

With no help of relief, Pemberton tried to negotiate with Grant. The Union general insisted on only unconditional surrender. That came on July 4, 1863, when the city's food and ammunition finally ran out. Grant's troops entered the city.

The map details the route taken by Union troops in their surprise assault on Vicksburg.

BATTLE DETAILS

1. In March–April 1863 Grant took his army south along the Union-held Louisiana side of the Mississippi. His 30,000 men crossed the river at Bruinsburg in David Porter's fleet of gunboats.

2. Grant's army moved northeast, fighting a series of battles. They captured Jackson, the state capital of Mississippi, on May 14.

3. Grant turned back west toward Vicksburg. He defeated Pemberton's troops at Champion's Hill and again at Big Black River before besieging the city. With supplies almost reduced to nothing, Pemberton surrendered on July 4, 1863.

AUGUST 17, SOUTH CAROLINA Union forces begin a bombardment of Fort Sumter in Charleston Harbor, the place where the first shots of the war were fired.

AUGUST 20, KANSAS William Quantrill's Confederate guerrillas attack Lawrence, killing more than 150 civilians and destroying 200 buildings.

SEPTEMBER 19–20, TENNESSEE Confederates win a hollow victory at the two-day Battle of Chickamauga, losing 18,000 to the Union's 16,000, and forcing only a partial Union withdrawal to Chattanooga.

SEPTEMBER 29, ITALY Troops led by the nationalist Giuseppe Garibaldi defeat a papal army, a major obstruction to Italian unification.

Battle of Gettysburg

The fighting at Gettysburg on July 1–3, 1863, was the largest and most famous battle of the Civil War. It marked the South's greatest advance into the North—and the beginning of its eventual defeat.

A drawing by Alfred Waud shows a Confederate attack on the second day of Gettysburg.

The origins of the battle lay in the decision of Confederate commander Robert E. Lee to invade the North for the second time. On June 16, 1863, about 75,000 men of the Army of Northern Virginia again crossed the Potomac. Lee's intention

1863
October–December

CIVIL WAR

OCTOBER 15, SOUTH CAROLINA
Confederate submarine *H.L. Hunley* sinks on its second test voyage, drowning all its crew.

NOVEMBER 19, PENNSYLVANIA
Lincoln makes his famous "Gettysburg Address" during the dedication of the cemetery on the battlefield.

OTHER EVENTS

OCTOBER 3, UNITED STATES
President Abraham Lincoln proclaims the last Thursday in November as Thanksgiving Day.

OCTOBER 23, SWITZERLAND
The first conference of the International Committee of the Red Cross is held.

NOVEMBER 23, UNITED STATES
A patent is granted to the first process for color photography.

October   November

was to meet the Army of the Potomac and defeat it in battle. Lee was under pressure for a rapid result. Union forces were besieging the strategically vital Confederate city of Vicksburg on the Mississippi River. He hoped that a decisive victory would force the Union to surrender before Vicksburg fell.

The battle begins

The war's largest battle began when a Confederate division foraging for supplies ran into a Union cavalry brigade near Gettysburg, Pennsylvania, early on July 1. The Union commander, John Buford, decided to hold the town while he sent word to the Army of the Potomac's new commander, General George G. Meade.

Gettysburg lay at the junction of roads that fanned out to Washington, Baltimore, and Harrisburg, the state capital. Both Meade and Robert E. Lee ordered their forces to concentrate on the town, making a battle inevitable.

Fighting began in the afternoon to the north of the town. Confederates pushed back the Union XI Corps, which eventually broke and fled back through the town. The North was rescued from complete disaster by the arrival of Winfield Scott Hancock and his II Corps. Hancock rallied the Union troops on Cemetery Hill. By the end of the first day the Confederates occupied Gettysburg itself. Despite their defeat,

Confederate troops use the huge boulders on Culp's Hill as cover during the Battle of Gettysburg.

NOVEMBER 23, TENNESSEE
The Battle of Chattanooga sees Union troops push back the Confederates.

NOVEMBER 24–25, TENNESSEE The Union capture of Chattanooga opens the "Gateway to the South."

DECEMBER 1, WASHINGTON, D.C.
Confederate spy Belle Boyd is freed from prison by Union authorities.

DECEMBER 9, TENNESSEE
After a 16-day siege, Confederate defenders withdraw from the town of Knoxville.

DECEMBER 16, TENNESSEE General Joseph Johnston takes command of the Confederate Army of Tennessee, replacing General William Hardee.

NOVEMBER 26, UNITED STATES
The first modern Thanksgiving Day is celebrated in the North.

DECEMBER 1, CHILE
A fire in a church causes panic in which 1,500 worshipers die.

A painting by Edwin Forbes shows Union troops on the summit of Little Round Top.

however, Union forces were now in a far stronger defensive position.

The second day

By July 2 Meade's 90,000 men were arranged in a shape that resembled a long fishhook. The Union line followed the high ground from Culp's Hill to Cemetery Hill and south along Cemetery Ridge. On the Confederate side, Lee now had three corps in position along Seminary Ridge.

Fighting began in the afternoon when Union general Daniel E. Sickles advanced from Cemetery Ridge against Meade's orders. Sickles's III Corps was destroyed in fierce fighting around the Peach Orchard and Devil's Den. His error had left the Union left flank exposed. Gouvernor K. Warren saw the danger and sent troops to occupy a hill known as Little Round Top, which dominated the position. He was just in time. A Confederate division reached the hill almost at the same time, but the Union defenders drove them off. On the Confederate left attacks on Cemetery Hill and Culp's Hill began in the early evening. When darkness fell, Meade still held his ground.

The decisive day

The next day, July 3, Lee was determined to break the Union center on Cemetery Ridge. If he could achieve a victory, he would win the battle—and perhaps even the war, because

GETTYSBURG

The town of Gettysburg was strategically important because it lay at the junction of roads running out to Washington and Baltimore to the south and east and to Harrisburg, the capital of Pennsylvania, to the north.

1864 January–March

CIVIL WAR

JANUARY 14, GEORGIA Union General William T. Sherman begins his infamous March through the South.

JANUARY 17, TENNESSEE At the Battle of Dandridge, Confederate forces repel Union troops from the Dandridge area.

FEBRUARY 9, VIRGINIA A total of 109 Union prisoners escape through a tunnel at Libby Prison in Richmond.

FEBRUARY 14–20, MISSISSIPPI In the Battle of Meridian, William T. Sherman leads a successful Union raid to destroy an important railroad junction.

OTHER EVENTS

FEBRUARY 1, DENMARK Prussian forces invade the Danish province of Schleswig, beginning the Second Schleswig War.

January   February

defeat would probably force the Union to surrender. At 1:00 P.M., 150 guns on Seminary Ridge began the biggest Confederate artillery bombardment of the war against the Union lines.

The guns fell silent at 3:00 P.M., and Lee sent forward his infantry. Led by George E. Pickett, some 15,000 men marched steadily across a mile (1.6 km) of open ground toward where Union defenders hid behind a stone wall.

Pickett's troops advanced into Union artillery fire, but continued to walk forward. The Union infantry fired volleys of musket fire. Only a handful of Confederates reached the stone wall.

Lee had made a huge tactical error. On July 4 he ordered his defeated army to withdraw. He had suffered 20,000 casualties, against the Union total of 23,000. The Confederacy never again threatened the Northern capital.

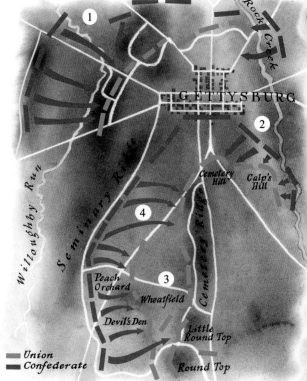

This map shows the movements of Union and Confederate troops over the terrible three-day battle.

BATTLE DETAILS

1. On July 1 Confederates pushed Union forces south through the town. They then occupied Gettysburg, while Union forces fell back to high ground to the south.

2. On July 2 the Union line came close to collapse in fierce fighting around the Devil's Den and Peach Orchard.

3. Toward nightfall, the Confederates launched uncoordinated attacks on Cemetery Hill and Culp's Hill.

4. On July 3, Lee ordered 15,000 infantry to make a frontal assault on Union lines. The advance, known as Pickett's Charge, was a disaster. It marked the effective end of the battle.

FEBRUARY 20, FLORIDA Many men of the 8th Regiment of United States Colored Troops are killed or injured in the Battle of Olustee near Jacksonville; Union forces retreat to the coast.

MARCH 2, THE NORTH Lieutenant General Ulysees S. Grant is made commander of all the armies of the United States.

MARCH 25, KENTUCKY Confederate cavalry attack the city of Paducah on the Ohio River; they retreat the next day, having suffered many casualties.

MARCH 14, AFRICA British explorers Samuel and Florence Baker discover Lake Albert at the headwaters of the Nile River.

March

Battle of Chickamauga

After victories at Gettysburg and Vicksburg, the Union hoped to deal
a final blow to the Confederacy at Chattanooga. In September 1863
the armies clashed at Chickamauga Creek, just outside the city.

At Chickamauga,
Bragg's Confederates
forced the Union
army into retreat.

Chattanooga, in southeastern Tennessee, was an important
Union target because it was a junction on the main
east–west railroad through the South. Its capture would further
divide the Confederacy. The Confederate Army of Tennessee

1864 April–June

CIVIL WAR

APRIL 12, TENNESSEE
Confederate troops massacre
the Union garrison at Fort
Pillow, killing 202 African
Americans.

APRIL 17, GEORGIA
Hungry citizens of
Savannah stage bread
riots over the lack of food.

MAY 3, VIRGINIA The Union
Army of the Potomac starts
to move south crossing the
difficult terrain of the
Wilderness region.

OTHER EVENTS

APRIL 10, MEXICO The
French declare Archduke
Maximilian of Austria to
be emperor of Mexico.

APRIL 22, UNITED STATES
Congress decides to print
the phrase "In God We
Trust" on U.S. coins.

MAY 9, NORTH SEA Austria
and Denmark fight a naval
battle at Heligoland during
the Second Schleswig War.

April   May

had been forced back to the city by the Union Army of the Cumberland in the Tullahoma Campaign of June 1863.

The Union commander, William S. Rosecrans, met little opposition as his army crossed the Tennessee River at several points south of Chattanooga. The advance forced the Confederate General Braxton Bragg to evacuate the city on September 7. Bragg withdrew to Lafayette in northern Georgia, where he concentrated his army for a counterattack.

A chance for Bragg

Rosecrans believed that Bragg was still in retreat and prepared to pursue him. Leaving behind a small force to guard Chattanooga, he moved his army of 62,000 men south into northern Georgia. During the advance, the Union's three corps became separated.

Bragg saw his opportunity to strike. He headed west to try to bring Union forces to battle. He also received reinforcements from the Army of Northern Virginia. He now commanded 65,000 men.

Sensing danger, Rosecrans went on the defensive. He ordered his army to return north toward Chattanooga. Rosecrans was worried that Bragg would cut him off from Chattanooga. On September 18 he ordered General George H. Thomas to position his

The Union line advances through the forest toward the Confederates at the Battle of Chickamauga.

MAY 5–6, VIRGINIA
Grant and Lee fight the inconclusive Battle of the Wilderness.

MAY 12, VIRGINIA
Grant and Lee fight again at the Battle of Spotsylvania. The battle is a draw.

JUNE 3, VIRGINIA
The Battle of Cold Harbor is a disaster for the Union army. They lose 7,000 men for no gain against Confederate losses of 1,500.

JUNE 27, GEORGIA
The Battle of Kennesaw Mountain sees Sherman's Union troops suffer heavy losses of 3,000 against Johnston's Confederate losses of 552.

MAY, GREAT BRITAIN
Charles Dickens publishes the first part of *Our Mutual Friend*.

MAY 26, UNITED STATES
Congress creates the territory of Montana, with its original capital at Virginia City.

JUNE 15, UNITED STATES Secretary of War Edwin M. Stanton creates Arlington National Cemetery, Virginia, on land previously owned by Confederate General Robert E. Lee.

Armies on the battlefield at Chickamauga, which was a natural amphitheater.

A NATURAL ENEMY

The Confederate and Union armies found themselves fighting a third enemy: the landscape. The battlefied at Chickamauga was a natural amphitheater, covered in places by thick forest. As the two sides set their battle lines, the dense vegetation stopped either from knowing that the other was just on the other side of the creek.

corps to prevent Bragg from performing such a maneuver.

Bragg did not realize that Thomas now formed the left flank of the Union army. He crossed his forces over Chickamauga Creek on September 18. He skirmished with two Union cavalry brigades before camping for the night.

The battle begins

Both the battle lines were now in position. The terrain along the creek was covered in woods and thick vegetation. Neither side was aware that the other was present. On the morning of September 19, a single Union division advanced. It believed that it had trapped a small Confederate force west of the creek. Instead, it sparked a full-scale battle.

In the confused fighting that broke out, both sides suffered heavy casualties. There was no decisive outcome, however. In the late afternoon, John Bell Hood's Confederates launched an

1864
July–September

CIVIL WAR

JULY 9, MARYLAND Confederates defeat Union troops at the Battle of Monocacy.

JULY 11, WASHINGTON, D.C. Facing strong Union defenses, Confederates withdraw from their attack.

JULY 22, GEORGIA Confederate General Hood's troops fail to defeat General Sherman's men at the Battle of Atlanta. Confederate losses are 8,000; Union losses are 3,600.

AUGUST 5, ALABAMA Union warships defeat Confederate vessels at the Battle of Mobile Bay: Union admiral David G. Farragut is said to have ordered, "Damn the torpedoes; full speed ahead!"

OTHER EVENTS

JULY 5, UNITED STATES The Bank of California is founded with holdings of $2 million.

JULY 14, UNITED STATES Gold is discovered in Montana at Helena, which will later become the state capital.

AUGUST 8, SWITZERLAND The first Geneva Convention is held to discuss the treatment of wounded soldiers in war.

July   August

attack that threatened to split the Union line, but at the last moment Rosecrans sent reinforcements to plug the gap.

Intending to spend the next day fighting on the defensive, Rosecrans ordered his men to dig trenches for protection. Meanwhile, Bragg planned an all-out attack that would force the Union army south, away from Chattanooga—and ultimately toward its destruction.

On the 20th, Confederate attacks originally made little headway against Thomas's position on the Union left. Then Rosecrans made a critical error. Mistakenly believing that there was a gap in his line to the north, he moved a division from the right of his line to plug it—and created a gap there.

Rosecrans' accidental opening of the gap coincided with an attack by three Confederate divisions led by James Longstreet. Before Rosecrans could correct his mistake, the Union's defensive position was shattered. Rosecrans was forced to order a retreat as Longstreet threatened to cut his line of communication with Chattanooga.

The price of victory

Chickamauga was a hollow victory for Bragg. He had lost more than 18,000 casualties but had not achieved the final defeat of the Army of the Cumberland. Bragg had succeed only in pushing Rosecrans back to Chattanooga. The Union army in Tennessee had survived to fight another day.

While Thomas fought for the Union, his family supported the Confederates.

THE ROCK OF CHICKAMAUGA

Not all Union forces were through fighting after Rosecrans ordered a retreat. Troops under George H. Thomas made a stand on Snodgrass Hill, a wooded ridge on the northern end of the Union line. In one of the war's most heroic defensive stands Thomas succeeded in holding Bragg at bay as Rosecrans and the bulk of the Union army withdrew into Chattanooga. For his efforts Thomas earned the Medal of Honor and was thereafter known as the "Rock of Chickamauga."

In stark contrast to Thomas, Union commander Rosecrans was inconsolable as he was carried along into Chattanooga by the wreckage of his army.

AUGUST 31, ILLINOIS The Democratic National Convention in Chicago nominates General George B. McClellan as its presidential candidate on an antiwar ticket.

SEPTEMBER 1, GEORGIA General Sherman cuts the last supply line to Atlanta, the railroad, forcing the Confederates to leave the city.

SEPTEMBER 16, VIRGINIA Confederate cavalrymen raid Union beef supplies on the James River to feed hungry Southerners.

SEPTEMBER 22, VIRGINIA Union forces defeat Confederates at the Battle of Fisher's Hill and start to destroy crops in the Shenandoah Valley.

SEPTEMBER 5, JAPAN British, Dutch, and French fleets attack Japan to open the Shimonoseki Straits to navigation.

SEPTEMBER 15, ITALY The new country gives up its claims to Rome; the Italians agree to make Florence their capital.

September

Battle of Chattanooga

After his victory at Chickamauga, Confederate General Braxton
Bragg besieged the Union Army of the Cumberland in the key
Tennessee city of Chattanooga.

A painting of the
Confederate attack
on Fort Sanders,
Tennessee, on
November 29, 1863.

Five months earlier, the commander of the Army of the
Cumberland, General William S. Rosecrans, had begun
capturing territory in central and eastern Tennessee. The Union
advance on Chattanooga in September 1863 had driven

1864
October–November

CIVIL WAR

OCTOBER 19, VIRGINIA
Union forces, under
General Sheridan, defeat
General Early's Confederate
Army of the Valley at the
Battle of Cedar Creek.

OCTOBER 26, ALABAMA
Union forces at Decatur prevent
Confederates led by John Bell
Hood from crossing the
Tennessee River in an attempt
to cut William T. Sherman's
lines of communication.

OCTOBER 27, VIRGINIA
Union forces assaulting
the Confederate capital
at Richmond are defeated
in the Second Battle of
Fair Oaks.

OTHER EVENTS

OCTOBER 11, UNITED STATES
Slavery is abolished
in Maryland.

OCTOBER 30, AUSTRIA The
Peace of Vienna ends the
Second Schleswig War between
Germany and Denmark.

OCTOBER 31, UNITED STATES
Nevada is admitted to the
Union as the 36th state.

October

Confederate General Braxton Bragg and his Confederate Army of Tennessee out of the city. Shortly afterward, however, Bragg had in turn halted the Union advance at the Battle of Chickamauga (September 19–20). Rosecrans was forced back into Chattanooga. Bragg then prepared to lay siege to the city to win it back.

This photograph shows the railroad at Chattanooga, with Lookout Mountain in the background.

Under siege

Chattanooga's strategic importance was clear to both sides. It stood at a junction on the vital Confederate railroad that linked Virginia with Tennessee, Georgia, and points west. For the Union, Chattanooga could be a base from which to capture Atlanta. As the war went on, it had become clear that whoever controlled Chattanooga would be in a position to control Tennessee, Georgia, and Alabama.

Now, however, Chattanooga had become a trap. The outlook for the Union forces was grim. President Abraham Lincoln sent additional Union troops to reinforce the city, but food and ammunition quickly began to run out. Bragg's Confederates were not strong enough to strike a fatal blow, however. When Union General Ulysses S. Grant arrived in October, he brought new hope to the defenders by restoring their supply lines. He also prepared to go on the offensive. Grant planned to push the Confederates from the fortifications around the city.

NOVEMBER 4, TENNESSEE
Confederate cavalry commander Nathan B. Forrest completes a 23-day raid in Georgia and Tennessee by destroying a Union supply base at Johnsonville.

NOVEMBER 15, GEORGIA
Union general William T. Sherman burns much of Atlanta before setting out on his notorious "March to the Sea."

NOVEMBER 25, NEW YORK
Confederate spies fail in a plot to burn down New York City.

NOVEMBER 8, UNITED STATES
Abraham Lincoln is reelected for a second term as president of the United States.

NOVEMBER 29, UNITED STATES
Militia in Colorado massacre some 200 Cheyenne and Arapaho at Sand Creek in retaliation for an attack on settlers.

This map shows the Confederate defensive line as the war began.

WESTERN THEATER

The Confederate defensive line at the beginning of the war stretched from the Mississippi River to the Cumberland Gap in the Appalachian foothills. The strategic importance of the rivers and railroads in the West meant that many major battles were fought west of the Appalachians.

Battle Above the Clouds

Grant's attempt to break the Confederate siege began on November 23, when the Army of the Cumberland crossed the Tennessee River in a number of places. In order to force Bragg out of his positions high above Chattanooga, elements of Grant's army scaled Lookout Mountain. On November 24 they fought units of Bragg's army on the slopes in what became known as the Battle Above the Clouds. The Union victory forced Bragg to give up a key position.

Missionary Ridge

Bragg withdrew his troops to Missionary Ridge, south of the Tennessee River. Bragg was let down by his generals, however, who placed their men poorly. Their errors enabled George H. Thomas to win a stunning victory on November 25, when his Union troops stormed and captured Missionary Ridge. With no safe positions left, Bragg's priority was to protect the key rail line to Atlanta, along which he retreated south.

Significant victory

The Confederate defense had not finished completely. On November 29, Confederates launched a futile attack on Fort Sanders, Tennessee, to stem the Union assault. The

1864–1865 December–January

CIVIL WAR

DECEMBER 13, GEORGIA
Union troops capture Fort McAllister near Savannah.

DECEMBER 15, TENNESSEE
At the Battle of Nashville, the Confederate Army of Tennessee is defeated by the Union Army of the Cumberland.

DECEMBER 20, GEORGIA
The Confederate garrison escapes from Savannah.

DECEMBER 21, GEORGIA
Sherman and his men enter Savannah unopposed at the conclusion of the "March to the Sea."

OTHER EVENTS

DECEMBER 8, VATICAN Pope Pius IX publishes the *Syllabus of Errors*, which condemns liberalism and reformism.

December

unsuccessful 20-minute attack left 780 Confederate casualties and ended in a humiliating withdrawal.

The battles for Chattanooga were over. After a six-month campaign, Union armies had finally been able to take control of the "Gateway to the South." The capture of the city changed the course of the war. It gave Union General William T. Sherman a supply base from which to launch the campaign against Atlanta planned for 1864. For the Confederacy, by contrast, defeat at Chattanooga sealed their loss of the rail networks, food supplies, and manpower of central Tennessee.

BATTLE DETAILS

1. On October 26 General Grant set up the "cracker" line to supply the besieged Army of the Cumberland inside Chattanooga.

2. On November 23 Union troops dislodged the Confederates from their position below Missionary Ridge.

3. In the "Battle Above the Clouds," Union troops drove away Confederate defenders from Lookout Mountain on November 24.

4. In a remarkable attack on November 25, Union forces routed Bragg's Confederates from Missionary Ridge.

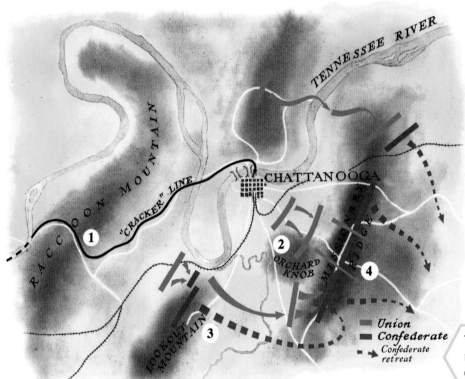

This map details the maneuvers of both sides during the battle.

JANUARY 15, NORTH CAROLINA
Wilmington, the last port in Confederate hands, is closed.

JANUARY 19, SOUTH CAROLINA
General Sherman vows to march through the Carolinas.

JANUARY 31, VIRGINIA
Robert E. Lee is named general-in-chief of all the Confederate armies.

JANUARY 4, UNITED STATES
The New York Stock Exchange opens its first permanent headquarters.

JANUARY 27, PERU
Peru's independence is established in a treaty with Spain.

JANUARY 31, UNITED STATES The House of Representatives approves an amendment to the Constitution abolishing slavery; it will become the Thirteenth Amendment.

Ulysses S. Grant

Ulysses Simpson Grant was vital to the Union victory at Chattanooga in November 1863. He went on to become general-in-chief of the Union armies, and their most outstanding commander.

Grant was famous for his lack of formality in both his behavior and his style of dress.

Grant had headed to Chattanooga after taking command of all Union forces west of the Appalachian Mountains on October 16, 1863. The Union victory that he masterminded the following month cemented his reputation. For much of the war,

1865
February–March

CIVIL WAR

FEBRUARY 3, VIRGINIA
President Lincoln and Confederate representatives fail to agree on a diplomatic ending to the war.

FEBRUARY 16, SOUTH CAROLINA
Columbia surrenders to General Sherman's Union troops.

FEBRUARY 17, SOUTH CAROLINA
As Union troops enter Columbia, someone sets fire to cotton bales across the town. Over half of the city is destroyed.

FEBRUARY 27, KENTUCKY
Confederate guerrilla leader William C. Quantrill and his band attack civilians in Hickman.

OTHER EVENTS

FEBRUARY 12, UNITED STATES
Henry Highland Garnet becomes the first African American to speak in the House of Representatives.

FEBRUARY 22, UNITED STATES
Tennessee adopts a new state constitution that outlaws slavery.

February

President Abraham Lincoln had been eager to find generals who were not too timid to fight. After Chattanooga, Lincoln made Grant general-in-chief of all the Union armies. In March 1864, Grant traveled to Washington, D.C., to receive the thanks of the U.S. Congress and his new promotion.

Unconventional record

The Union's new supreme commander had a mixed record. Grant had graduated from the U.S. Military Academy at West Point and served in the Mexican War (1846–1848). But his military career had been spoiled by rumors of drunkenness and he resigned in 1854. He did not find much more success in life as a civilian. The businesses he started failed. By the time war broke out in 1861, Grant was working as a clerk in the family store. When he offered his services to the War Department, he was refused.

It was only with political backing that Grant was given command of the 21st Illinois Volunteers. Soon he was promoted to brigadier general and given command of the District of Southeast Missouri.

Mixed fortunes

In February 1862, Grant won his first major success. He captured Fort Donelson, in Tennessee. Grant's victory

Artist Winslow Homer followed the Army of the Potomac, drawing ordinary soldiers like this drummer and bugler.

MARCH 2, VIRGINIA
The Shenandoah Valley is in Union control after the Confederates lose the Battle of Waynesboro.

MARCH 3, WASHINGTON, D.C. The U.S. Congress sets up the Freedmen's Bureau to help deal with the problems resulting from the sudden freeing of tens of thousands of slaves.

MARCH 13, RICHMOND
The Confederate Congress passes a law authorizing the use of black troops.

MARCH 19, NORTH CAROLINA
Joseph E. Johnston attempts to stop the march of Union general William T. Sherman through the Carolinas in the Battle of Bentonville; he is defeated late the following day.

MARCH 4, UNITED STATES
Abraham Lincoln is inaugurated for his second term as president.

MARCH 18, SOUTH AMERICA
Paraguay goes to war with the Triple Alliance of Brazil, Argentina, and Uruguay.

A NATION'S HERO

Hailed as the nation's hero, Grant was promoted to full general in 1866. In 1868 he was elected the 18th U.S. president, but his two terms were marred by several scandals. His reputation was restored by his memoirs of the Civil War, which he completed only a week before his death in 1885.

showed his tactical brilliance. His refusal to accept anything other than the unconditional surrender of the fort showed his aggressiveness. Grant quickly became a hero in the North.

Again, however, Grant's reputation soon suffered. In April 1862, he led a Union army to Pittsburg Landing on the Tennessee River. In the Battle of Shiloh on April 6, Grant was taken completely by surprise by a Confederate attack. He only avoided defeat thanks to substantial reinforcements. Following the Battle of Shiloh, Grant fought with his superior, Henry W. Halleck, and was removed from field command. But his aggressiveness had already won the attention of Lincoln, who soon had him reinstated.

A turning point

In October 1862, Lincoln put Grant in command of the Army of the Tennessee. Grant's first objective was Vicksburg, the city that controled the lower Mississippi River. Grant made a daring advance on Vicksburg in a combined operation with navy gunboats that sailed down the river. Grant laid siege to Vicksburg, which finally surrendered on July 4, 1863. The victory was a turning point for Grant, who was promoted to major general.

On October 16, 1863, Grant took command of all Union forces from the

Ulysses S. Grant (standing center in front of a tree) with his staff in 1864.

1865
April–May

CIVIL WAR

APRIL 1, VIRGINIA
The Battle of Five Forks ends in defeat for the Confederate Army of Northern Virginia.

APRIL 2, VIRGINIA
Grant attacks Petersburg and the Confederates start a retreat from Petersburg and Richmond.

APRIL 6, VIRGINIA
Lee loses 8,000 men to Union attacks at the Battle of Sayler's Creek.

APRIL 7, VIRGINIA
Grant asks Lee for his army's surrender; Lee asks for terms.

APRIL 9, VIRGINIA
Lee surrenders to Ulysses S. Grant at Appomattox Courthouse.

OTHER EVENTS

April

Mississippi River to the Appalachian Mountains. His first action was to help win the victory at Chattanooga, Tennessee.

Grant's strategy relied on the North's superior resources. He knew that he could grind down the Confederate armies in costly battles. He also intended to weaken the South by destroying its farmlands.

In May 1864 Grant set out for Richmond, Virginia, with the Army of the Potomac, under George G. Meade. The six-week Overland Campaign cost the Union 60,000 casualties, but Grant kept moving forward. Eventually he forced the Confederate commander Robert E. Lee back to Petersburg, which Grant besieged for 10 months.

Grant is inaugurated as U.S. president in 1869. He was to prove a better soldier than politician.

Grant's final victory

Grant's junior, William T. Sherman, meanwhile, left Atlanta and marched through Georgia to the sea. His men destroyed Confederate supply lines, along with farms and homes.

On April 2, 1865, Lee withdrew from Petersburg, and Richmond was evacuated. After a running fight, Grant cornered Lee at Appomattox. He accepted Lee's surrender, while granting his enemy generous terms of surrender.

GRANT AT APPOMATTOX

Grant described his feelings on the day of Robert E. Lee's surrender on April 9, 1865.

"We greeted each other ... What General Lee's feelings were I do not know. As he was a man of much dignity, with an impassable face, it was impossible to say ... but my own feelings, which had been quite jubilant ... were sad and depressed. I felt like anything rather than rejoicing at the downfall of a foe who had fought so long and valiantly, and had suffered so much for a cause, though that was, I believe, one of the worst for which a people had ever fought, and one for which there was the least excuse."

APRIL 14, WASHINGTON, D.C. President Lincoln is shot while watching a play at the theater.

APRIL 15, WASHINGTON, D.C. Lincoln dies from his injuries; Vice-President Andrew Johnson becomes president.

APRIL 26, NORTH CAROLINA Confederate General Joseph E. Johnston surrenders to General William T. Sherman.

MAY 10, GEORGIA Confederate President Jefferson Davis is captured and taken into custody.

MAY 29, WASHINGTON, D.C. President Andrew Johnson grants an amnesty and pardon to Confederate soldiers who will take an oath of allegiance to the Constitution.

APRIL 21, UNITED STATES Lincoln's funeral train leaves Washington, D.C.; it will popularize the Pullman sleeping car.

APRIL 27, TENNESSEE 2,000 Union soldiers aboard the riverboat *Sultana* die when it catches fire and sinks on the Mississippi River.

MAY 1, UNITED STATES Walt Whitman publishes "Drum Taps," his long poem about the Civil War.

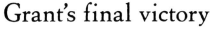

NEED TO KNOW

Some of the subjects covered in this book feature in many state curricula. These are topics you should understand.

People:
Abraham Lincoln
Robert E. Lee
Thomas "Stonewall" Jackson
Ulysses S. Grant

Strategy:
Siege Warfare
Invasion of the North
Union Cavalry Improvement
Guerrilla Warfare

Politics:
Emancipation Proclamation
Military Draft
Bread Riots in the South
Life Under Occupation

KNOW THIS

This section summarizes two major themes of this book: the political background of the fighting and the strategies of the North and the South.

POLITICS

EMANCIPATION PROCLAMATION

Lincoln's Emancipation Proclamation came into effect on January 1, 1863. It declared all slaves held in rebel states to be free. The war was now a struggle to destroy slavery and free the slaves.

ABRAHAM LINCOLN

A combination of the Emancipation Proclamation and improved news from the battlefield strengthened Lincoln's position: he had been criticized for abusing his presidential power.

FREEDMEN

The government set up Freedmen's Bureaus to look after liberated slaves. Many Northern commanders and soldiers did not like black Americans and treated freed slaves badly, even if they were in military service.

FOREIGN RELATIONS

At the start of the war, countries such as France and Great Britain had said that they would remain neutral. The South had hoped that, if it was successful on the battlefield, foreign countries would recognize the independence of the Confederacy. The Emancipation Proclamation meant this could no longer happen: no European country would be seen to back a struggle to keep slavery.

STRATEGY

• The North continued to try to deny the South resources. Its blockade remained in force and it made new efforts to win control of the Mississippi.
• The North besieged the key towns of Port Hudson and Vicksburg.
• Vicksburg was the point that held both halves of the Confederacy together; if it fell, the South would be split in two.
• The death of Thomas "Stonewall" Jackson at the Battle of Chancellorsville was a blow to Confederate morale; Lee lost one of his best commanders.
• Lee planned to invade the North in the hope of delivering a knock-out blow to the Union before it could capture Vicksburg.
• The North's victory at the Battle of Gettysburg ended Lee's advance and Southern hopes of capturing Washington, D.C. It was called the "high-water mark of the Confederacy."

TEST YOURSELF

These questions will help you discover what you have learned from this book.
Check the pages listed in the answers below.

1. **What Union victory gave Abraham Lincoln the chance to make the Emancipation Proclamation?**

2. **What Amendment to the U.S. Constitution finally ended slavery?**

3. **How was General Joseph Hooker known in the North?**

4. **Why was the victory at Chancellorsville a disaster for the South?**

5. **What convinced General Franklin Gardner to surrender Port Hudson to Union forces?**

6. **What was important about the Battle of Brandy Station?**

7. **How did Ulysses S. Grant get his army across the Mississippi at Vicksburg?**

8. **How many Confederates set out on Pickett's Charge?**

9. **How many states did Chattanooga give control over?**

10. **What spoiled Ulysses S. Grant's early career in the U.S. Army?**

ANSWERS

1. Antietam (Sharpsburg) (see page 8). 2. Thirteenth Amendment, 1865 (see page 9). 3. "Fighting Joe" (see page 13). 4. Because Stonewall Jackson was shot by his own side and fatally wounded (see page 15). 5. The surrender of Vicksburg (see page 19). 6. It showed the dramatic improvement of the Union cavalry (see page 23). 7. On Union gunboats (see page 26). 8. 15,000 (see page 31). 9. Three: Tennessee, Georgia, and Alabama (see page 37). 10. Rumors that he drank too much (see page 41).

GLOSSARY

artillery Heavy guns such as cannons that fire shells and balls a long way.

batteries Groups of heavy guns, such as cannons.

bayonet A sharp dagger that is attached to the end of a rifle for hand-to-hand fighting.

blockade Measures aimed at preventing trade by using ships to intercept vessels heading toward port.

bombardment A period of artillery fire aimed at a particular target.

brigade A military unit made up of about 5,000 soldiers divided into two to six regiments.

cavalry Soldiers that fight on horseback.

counterattack An attack launched on the enemy after he has already attacked.

division The largest unit of an army: it is made up of three or four brigades.

entrench To dig in to a defensive position.

flank The side of a military unit or line.

fortifications Positions that are protected by strong defenses such as trenches or walls.

garrison A group of soldiers who occupy a military post.

infantry Soldiers who fight on foot.

ironclad A ship that is protected by a covering of iron armor.

militia Part of a country's army made up of citizens who are called on to serve in times of emergency.

regiment A military unit; at full strength, a regiment had 10 companies of 100 men.

rout A total defeat.

siege A military attack in which an army or city is surrounded and cut off in order to force its surrender.

skirmish A minor fight between enemy forces.

strategic Something that is important to an overall plan, even if it is not very important on its own.

FURTHER READING

BOOKS

Abnett, Dan. *Gamble for Victory: Battle of Gettysburg* (Graphic History). Osprey Publishing, 2006.

Beller, Susan Provost. *Billy Yank and Johnny Reb: Soldiering in the Civil War*. Twenty-First Century Books, 2007.

Burgan, Michael. *The Battle of Gettysburg* (Graphic Library, Graphic History). Capstone Press, 2006.

Champlin, John D. *Young Folk's History of the War For the Union*. British Library, 2011.

Champlin, Tim. *Snatching the General* (Chasing the Golden Treasure). Kindle Edition, 2011.

Colimore, Edward. *Eyewitness Reports: The Inquirer's Live Coverage of the American Civil War*. Philadelphia Inquirer, 2004.

Crane, Stephen. *The Red Badge of Courage*. Simon & Schuster, 2005.

Ernst, Kathleen. *Ghosts of Vicksburg*. White Mane Publishing Company, 2003.

King, David C. *The Triangle Histories of the Civil War: Battles—Battle of Chatanooga*. Blackbirch Press, 2002.

Myers, Walter Dean. *Riot*. Egmont USA, 2009.

Osborne, May Pope. *My America: My Brother's Keeper: Virginia's Civil War Diary, Book One*. Scholastic, 2002.

Stanchak, John E. *Eyewitness Civil War*. Dorling Kindersley, 2011.

Warren, Andrea. *Under Siege!: Three Children at the Civil War Battle for Vicksburg*. Melanie Kroupa Books, 2009.

WEBSITES

www.civilwar.com
Comprehensive privately run, moderated site on the Civil War.

www.civil-war.net
Collection of images, written sources, and other material about the Civil War.

www.historyplace.com/civilwar
The History Place Civil War timeline.

www.pbs.org/civilwar
PBS site supporting the Ken Burns film The Civil War.

www.civilwar.si.edu
The Smithsonian Institution's Civil War collections, with essays, images, and other primary sources.

INDEX